A Fireside Book published by Simon & Schuster

Angels from Hell

Almost Totally True Tales of Infernal,
and Otherwise Inexplicable,
Intervention

Jan Werner

ILLUSTRATED BY AUSTIN HUGHES AND GIDEON KENDALL

Fireside

Rockefeller Center
1230 Avenue of the Americas
New York, NY 10020

Designed by Gretchen Achilles
Manufactured in the United States of America

1   3   5   7   9   10   8   6   4   2

Library of Congress Cataloging-in-Publication Data
Werner, Jan, date.
Angels from hell : almost totally true tales of infernal, and
otherwise inexplicable, intervention / Jan Werner : illustrated by
Austin Hughes and Gideon Kendall.
          p.   cm.
      1. Angels—Humor.   I. Title.
         PN6162.W4524   1998
            818'.5407—dc21
           ISBN 0-684-83792-7

Acknowledgments

$\mathcal{T}$his book began as a tiny seed sprouting in the rich, damp soil of my thoughts; that soil, like any other, needed enrichment to become fertile. So many, many, many wonderful people contributed to that enrichment, and I'd like to thank a few of them here for creating such a fragrant and steaming compost heap for me.

Special, angel-frosted love to the Überangels, my family of origin—Ron, Pat, Stan, Natica, and Baby Werner ♡ Cassandra, my very own one-woman Psychic Friends Network ♡ Jack and Alie, who helped me see that mood disorders can be fun ♡ Amy, who's listened to so many tales of Loss, Frustration, Irritation and Humiliation that her Boredom tolerance must be virtually infinite ♡ the Angelic Guinea Pigs: Florence, Jocelyn, and Sloane ♡ My beloved animal companions—Jupiter, who lifts my spirits even more often than he lifts his leg, and Amarilla, who schooled me in the transitory nature of material objects by methodically chewing up almost everything I own ♡ Betsy Herman, my editor, who had the wit and foresight to offer me a contract ♡ Matt Walker, Betsy's assistant, who had the wit and forbearance to laugh at my jokes ♡ Austin Hughes and Gideon Kendall, whose drawings capture the sticky-sweet-yet-scary essence of the Angels from Hell ♡ The countless friends, acquaintances, and family members whose stories I've shamelessly appropriated for my own purposes ♡ And you, the person reading this right now, provided you actually cough up the cash to purchase a copy (or two).

～～～～～～～～～～～～～～～～～

✺

This book is dedicated with

love, joy, harmony, peace, bliss,

fellowship and mirth

to all the gentle souls who have seen

a hushed, sparkly glimmering at the edge of their

vision and wondered,

"Have I just glimpsed an angel,

or am I getting a migraine?"

The Angels from Hell are with you.

✺

～～～～～～～～～～～～～～～～～

Contents

Introduction

Today, angel lore blossoms like a tremendous rose that spreads its petals ever wider, eagerly awaiting the fuzzy bee of hope that will sprinkle the pollen of love through the weedy garden of fear. Angels are everywhere—perched on lapels, dangling from earrings, adorning rearview mirrors, peeping out of every nook and cranny like so many golden-haired, rosy-cheeked cockroaches. And every day, people call out for help from their own personal angels: love angels, job angels, house angels, transmission angels, thinner-thighs angels. Often, these prayers are answered. But, sometimes, sadly, they are not.

Why is this? If there is someone (or Someone, or Lots of Someones) looking out for us, why do irritating, annoying, humiliating, and just plain bad things keep happening to us? Are our angels lazy, or incompetent, or inattentive? Or are they doing this on purpose? What do these angels have against us, anyway? Should we take it personally, or what?

We must remember that Lucifer, too, is an angel. Once upon a time, he was the most radiantly beautiful angel in all of Heaven, cherished and admired by all, shimmering and glowing and oozing with holy effusions. But then—just like certain people we knew in high school—he became too proud. Stuck up, even. And that's why God banished him to the nether regions, the underworld, the place where there is no joy, no laughter, no sunshine, no aromatherapy. There, Lucifer gathered his own angels about him, and these angels—the Angels from Hell—are every bit as busy as the other angels, even if they tend to operate on a slightly smaller scale.

For every angel who leads us to our lost car keys, there is one who hides the remote control in the vegetable crisper. For every angel who drives us safely home, and finds a new shortcut, after we faint behind the wheel, there is an angel who crashes our hard drive at six o'clock the evening before the report is due. For every angel who guides the Amtrak conductor through successful open-heart surgery on our cousin after she keels over in the bar car, there's the angel who lovingly nurtures an enormous pimple that sprouts to throbbing life between our eyebrows on the morning of our Date of a Lifetime, causing us to make a mid-meal retreat to the restroom in Café des Artistes to apply cold poultices, where we discover more of the angel's handiwork in the form of a swag of spinach festively draped across one bicuspid, which so unnerves us that we return to the table without noticing the angel's piéce de resistance, a four-foot toilet paper streamer tenderly attached to our left heel, all of which leads our date to smile and say, "I'll be right back," only to disappear altogether and, as we later discover, move to another city and obtain an unlisted phone number.

We should not view these events as random cruelties—banal and meaningless misfortunes, mindless vicissitudes of an uncaring universe locked in an entropic spiral. Instead, we should think of these incidents as loving and corrective swats on the behind from the inconsistent, slightly scary Parent of Us All. Yes, there are lessons to be learned from the most unfortunate occurrence; we need only squint closely and hold our breath to detect the glimmering Spiritual Rolex that somehow was flushed down into the percolating Septic Tank of Life.

The stories contained in this volume are all true tales of encounters with beings from Beyond, or Below. Each of these events actually happened, to friends or relatives of mine, although I have taken the liberty of editing and rewriting a bit (for dramatic effect, or to keep from getting sued). Think of these stories as not merely true, but *better* than true—just like the reenactments on *Unsolved Mysteries*.

Perhaps you will find these little narratives instructive and inspiring. Or perhaps you will merely thank your own Higher Power that none of your experiences is included here. In any event, I hope that you will come away from this volume uplifted and refreshed, with room in your soul and light in your heart and blessedly empty space in your mind to take in the lessons presented by your very own, very special Angels from Hell.

14

The Angels of
Loss

Life is loss, and loss is life. We lose and lose and lose throughout life, until we lose even life. How would we know we truly had something if we never lost it? When you hold your breath, it does you no good—you must let it go, unless you're trying to make a point. So, in a sense, when we "lose" something, we actually "have" it. This is what the angels teach us.

The Angels Take an Unscheduled Flight

My dear grandmother (a sweet and spry widow) lived for many years in El Paso, Texas. Granny had two wee animal companions: her chihuahuas, Chiquita and Blanquita, which she always referred to as "my little angels." She fed them from her plate, let them sleep on their own little pillows in her bed, and drove them everywhere she went. "Love me, love my dogs"—that was Granny's motto.

Only two thorns pricked the tender flesh of Granny's golden years.

First, her children and their families had moved eight hundred miles away, to central Texas. This required many long drives across the majestic terrain of West Texas, which, for all its spatial grandeur, offers distressingly little in the way of visual stimuli.

Since Granny loved to drive, this would not have been a thorn at all but for the presence of her second thorn, which was the fact that Granny was prone to unexpected naps. Without warning, she'd fall sound asleep—at the dinner table, halfway through a piano recital, in the middle of *Murder, She Wrote* or *America's Funniest Home Videos*. We learned not to rouse her rudely, but to let her be. She'd wake up on her own a few minutes later, we'd explain how Jessica unveiled the killer of that nasty cranberry farmer, and that would be that.

But occasionally, especially on long drives, Granny would fall asleep behind the wheel. She would wake from one of her naps to find her motor home stuck on a saguaro, or the Thunderbird that replaced the motor home entangled in a barbed-wire fence. No one was ever injured in these little mishaps, but they did provoke much comment from the family (and Granny's insurance company).

Granny, however, was descended from resourceful and intrepid pioneer stock. She and the dogs kept right on traveling across the desert, and she cultivated the habit of stopping frequently for little naps, which kept her alert and on the highway.

One brilliant summer day, with the desert sky as expansive as a Wal-Mart parking lot, Granny pulled into a rest area midway through a typical journey. She walked Chiquita and Blanquita, then tied their leashes to the bumper so they could take the air while she enjoyed a nourishing snack of deviled eggs and pimento-cheese-and-celery boats. (Granny never traveled without a plentiful supply of provisions.) After this meal and her forty winks, she was refreshed and ready to resume her trip.

As Granny pulled back onto the interstate, a driver coming into the rest area honked at her. Granny waved, pleased by his pleasantry. As this greeting became a veritable shower of honking horns and wildly gesticulating drivers on the highway, though, Granny became slightly annoyed. She glanced into the rearview mirror, thinking some pesky auto part might have worked itself loose. That was when Granny received the shock of her life. Tiny Chiquita and tinier

Loss

Blanquita—leashes still firmly tied to the bumper, rhinestone harnesses glittering in the happy sun— were spinning aloft in the backdraft of the roaring Impala.

"Well, of course I stopped right away," she explained later, "and I was just scared to death to even get out of the car to check on the poor little darlings. And the strangest thing is, I know I put my baby girls back in the car. I just can't explain it." Clearly, the work of her Angels from Hell.

Fortunately, Chiquita and Blanquita were uninjured by their unscheduled flight. Granny told us the story in our breakfast room, while the dogs stared dolefully and reproachfully up at her, and we fondly laughed ourselves sick. Indeed, the only lasting effect of the incident was that Chiquita and Blanquita's tiny faces became (and remained) even more pop-eyed than before.

A shocking and inexplicable event, so near to disaster, became a very valuable lesson for Granny. "Those sweet little things don't even leave my side anymore. I had myself a little belt made, with rhinestones just like theirs—it's real cute—and I just clip their leashes right to it. I'm not taking a chance on losing them again."

꙯

Can dogs fly? Can paper fold itself into an airplane? Can flies drive? Only with faith, which stretches the safety net like firemen waiting for the fat lady to jump.

꙯

Think of all the objects you've lost over the years. Think of them coming together and tracking you down, pounding on your door, demanding to be let in. That plaid plastic lunchbox, your tenth-grade civics textbook, that lime-green velour turtleneck from last season, hundreds of small-appliance warranty cards, thousands of socks, billions of pens. Where would you put them all? What would your landlord say? Do you really want them back? Now say goodbye and let them go, this time forever.

Sometimes, just like the writers for TV detective shows, the angels hide clues in plain sight. When we rearrange the letters in "goodbye," what is the result? "Obey dog." And "bed go, yo." And "body ego." Could the lessons be any clearer?

In the fall, the leaves "fall," and take their "leave." Nature is so blessedly wise.

Is there a Grand Celestial Lint Trap that collects the fuzzy little leavings that are lost as we tumble in the Oversized Dryer of Life? To this question, we can only answer . . . maybe.

The Angels
Tend Bar

My dear friend Lorelei related this story to me in a dressing room at Loehmann's.

A few years ago, in what she now refers to as her larval stage, Lorelei was smitten with a dashing tattooed bard, a poet of the wa-wa pedal, a swain with a Strat—in short, a musician.

The relationship ended as relationships with musicians often do. One Thursday, Spiff said, "Look, babe, it's like they say. If you love something, you gotta let it go free. You got twenty bucks I can borrow?"

That Saturday, Lorelei's friend Bettina called with a fateful invitation.

Bettina's friend Biff was hosting a party, and Bettina insisted that Lorelei attend. "You've been mooning over that loser Spiff long enough," Bettina observed. "Come and meet some new guys."

Lorelei actually had been looking forward to sitting around in her bathrobe, watching reruns of *The X-Files* and eating a pint or two of Cherry Garcia low-fat frozen yogurt—a Saturday night of *not* jamming herself into some shiny black spandex-fortified ensemble, *not* treating Spiff and everyone else at some lame showcase to beers, and *not* coming home at six in the morning plagued with tinnitus. She *wanted* to stay home. Besides, Spiff had dumped her only two days ago, and she wanted time to mourn her loss. But Bettina persuaded Lorelei that she had to get right back on the horse that bit her, so to speak, and Lorelei found herself agreeing to attend the party.

Biff and his roommate, Chip, had come up with the clever notion of hosting a margarita-tasting party. Biff's father was a large-ish cheese in an appliance-store chain, and thus the boys had procured dozens of blenders, all of which they'd set a-whirr, each filled with a different concoction. When Bettina and Lorelei arrived, Chip greeted them with a foaming yellow pitcher.

"Creamed-corn margarita? I made it myself!"

No one would touch the creamed-corn potion, and there weren't many takers on Biff's brainstorm, a guacamole version. (Biff felt the idea had potential as a happy-hour special, efficiently combining several popular taste sensations in one chunky libation. Even he, however, had to admit that including the chips had been a culinary gaffe.) The lettuce margarita, though, was inoffensive; the peanut-butter margarita was intriguing; and the green-olive-and-pimento margarita had surprising body and an insouciant, ineffable charm. After much sampling, Bettina settled on the strawberry Jell-O margarita as her favorite; she likened it to "mangled gummy bears with a kick." Lorelei, more of a traditionalist, stuck to blueberry margaritas.

An hour or two (and a margarita or six) into the evening, Lorelei found herself engaged in lively conversation with a young man who seemed to be unattached, heterosexual, and not obviously psychopathic. Lorelei chatted him up with some enthusiasm, favoring him with her views on the local music scene, the intricacies of the new filing system she was devising at work, the really tragic dearth of decent manicure parlors in her neighborhood, and other issues of import. Lorelei unburdened herself as she hadn't in the weeks she'd been with Spiff, who had talked to his bandmates when he and Lorelei were out at clubs and practiced his three favorite guitar chords when they were alone.

At last, Lorelei felt the inevitable call of nature, and excused herself to "powder her nose." As she was washing her hands, she smiled broadly, thrilled at her social triumph—and felt her jaw plummet toward the sink. Her gums (upper and lower) were framed darkly with what looked like rock-n-roll eyeliner, making her vaguely resemble an extra from *Deliverance*. Upon closer inspection, the outline proved to be indigo bits of blueberry skin and seeds, attracted to her gums as if by static electricty—or Hellish design.

Lorelei crept out of the bathroom, found her purse, slipped out of the apartment unnoticed, and walked home.

"What was I thinking?" Lorelei now says. "I wasn't fit for human consumption. Okay, so Spiff was a loser, but losing a loser is still a loss, right? Not in the long run, maybe, but still. Now I know—sometimes it's better to stay home and lose a chance to meet someone than go out and end up losing your . . . your whatchamacallit . . . your self-esteem. Right?"

Were truer words ever spoken?

※

Sometimes we bob listlessly through life, like a teabag in a sun-tea jar. Sometimes we whirl furiously, like a margarita in a blender. Do we ever learn that life is like a backwards Bond martini—best enjoyed stirred, not shaken?

Perhaps the important things we've "lost" are not truly "gone." Instead, they are resting quietly and restfully, just out of sight, behind the Great Sofa Cushion of the Universe.

Before you blame a thief, check your pockets for holes.

What is loss, but Life's giggly way of providing us with glimmering opportunities to get new stuff?

"Eons ago," the angels whisper, "when the world was as young and frail and surly as a supermodel, humans had horns. Big, ugly, scabby-looking ones, sticking straight up from the tops of your heads. The horns kept getting caught in vines and bumping against low cave ceilings, and many, many humans inadvertently poked out loved ones' eyes in a badly navigated embrace. Slowly, the horns were lost. The human expression 'You have a point' is the only reminder of this faraway time. You see—loss is *good*."

The angels have a point.

The Angels Provide
Cat Care

A few years ago, my friend Miranda experienced this brush with her Angels from Hell.

Shortly after graduation from college, Miranda moved to Manhattan to embark upon her glamorous career as a painter—or maybe a writer, but then again she was really interested in acting, too, and she'd always loved fashion (people said she had a really unique style), so she didn't want to rule that out either. While Miranda was waiting to be discovered, she worked at a hushed and sepulchural Shrine to Art—a SoHo gallery. The coolness quotient of her job was high, and the salary was correspondingly low. Miranda's paychecks were so minuscule that she might as well have been paid in rubber bands, or toothpicks, or poker chips. Since her *real* parents (the vastly wealthy ones whom she was sure had set up a massive trust fund for her, but wouldn't dream of interfering with her relationship with the perfectly lovely but regrettably middle-class people who'd raised her) still had not made their presence known to her, Miranda experienced perpetual financial problems.

The first Christmas she lived in New York, Miranda made a bold assertion of her independence and refused to go home for the holidays. This would be the first time since she'd moved to the city that she would have the apartment to herself; all four girls with whom she shared the one-bedroom domicile would be away. Simultaneous with this decision, Beryl—a friend of a friend of a friend—came to Miranda with a business proposition: she had a Persian kitten named Tapioca, and would be traveling over the holidays. Would Miranda be willing to take care of the kitty? The fee would be $250.

Naturally, Miranda jumped at the chance. The night before Beryl's departure, she took the subway to the Upper West Side to collect her charge. Two hours later, Miranda cabbed it back to the Lower East Side, laden not only with cash, cat carrier, and cat food, but also a substantial tote bag full of cat toys, cat treats, cat vitamins, cat bed, cat perch, cat wardrobe, cat schedule, cat accessories, and cat emergency numbers, including those for a cat astrologer and a cat manicurist.

Miranda had nothing against cats as a species, but she would never have described herself as a "cat person." And she took an immediate dislike to Tapioca himself, despite the fact that Beryl clearly loved the snotty little dustmop. She ought to, Miranda reflected; Beryl had confided that she'd purchased Tapioca from a top breeder for $1,000. Clearly, Beryl was an idiot, but Miranda was perfectly willing to take her money.

When she reached home, Miranda slung the cat bag onto the kitchen counter, tossed the cat bed on the floor, opened the door of the cat carrier, bade Tapioca *bonne nuit,* and went to bed.

The next morning, Miranda woke early (shortly before noon), ready to enjoy her first day alone in the apartment. She played her favorite tape on the stereo, commandeered the TV remote control, and sloshed in the tub as long as she wanted. Only after Miranda had prepared Tapioca's breakfast, though, did she realize that the cat was nowhere in evidence.

She looked in the carrier. Empty. Nothing in the cat bed. Nothing under the sofa, under the bookshelves, in the compost heap of dirty clothes, or anywhere else she looked. Then, Miranda saw a sight that chilled her blood.

An open window.

The super, apparently a sauna enthusiast, cranked up the heat to such a degree that it was necessary to leave at least one window open all winter. Miranda had neglected to close that window after releasing Tapioca.

Scarcely daring to look, she crept to the sill and peered out. There was a tiny reprieve: no fluffy, flat-faced corpse in the courtyard.

Fueled by remorse and panic, Miranda tore through the apartment, upending every piece of poorly assembled Ikea furniture, tearing every tatty item out of the inadequate and improvised storage spaces. No Tapioca.

She sat on the living room/kitchen floor, trying to gather her wits. I'll buy a cat double, she thought. But two problems immediately presented themselves: first, she barely remembered what Tapioca looked like; and second, she didn't have a thousand pennies, much less a thousand dollars. Miranda thought of the vast sums of money that Beryl possessed. She thought of Beryl's extreme emotional distress. She thought of lawsuits, jail terms, and eternal ignominy.

In tears, Miranda threw on a coat and boots and staggered out into the street. She shuffled through snow drifts, past alarmed street denizens, into shadowy bodegas, wailing, "Tapioca! Tapioca! C'mere, baby! Tapioca! Tapioca! Where *are* you?! Tapioca!"

Hours later, drenched and chilled, Miranda returned to the apartment. In despair she collapsed in the kitchen/bathroom, rolling about on the floor and weeping hopelessly. Then, in mid-flail, something caught her eye: a bit of fluff and two shiny eyes at the very back of the two-inch crevice between the kitchen sink cabinet/storage unit and the dining table/ironing board/stove. *Tapioca!*

It took several hours and several cans of tuna, but Miranda finally lured Tapioca from his lair. She prostrated herself before him and swore that she would never, ever disparage him or his kind, by word or deed, ever again.

Tapioca remained quite content through the remainder of his visit, and returned uptown three pounds heavier.

As for Miranda, she soon was driven out of her neighborhood by the incessant cries of "You want tapioca? Yo, baby, I got tapioca for you!" that followed her whenever she left her apartment. She eventually settled in a well-known spiritual center in the southwestern United States and established her own felinocentric religion incorporating elements of Native American worship. High Priestess Mmmrrrrroww, as she is now known, describes herself as "living in a state of purrful bliss," and for this she thanks her Angels from Hell.

When cats hack up a beloved hairball, do they mourn their loss? Who are we to say that *our* losses—of time, money, a loved one, a limb—are more significant?

We are overjoyed when we lose weight, and distressed when we lose hair. Isn't the human spirit an odd and inconsistent little beast?

"Loss" rhymes with "moss." And "toss," and "floss," and "emboss," and "Hieronymus Bosch" (more or less). What is there to fear from such a friendly word?

Sometimes, when we say we have "lost" something, we do not mean "lost" as in "gone forever, never to return, so long, sayonara, kiss it bye-bye." Sometimes we mean "lost" as in "It's here somewhere, I just saw it, why the hell am I the only one who ever picks up around here anyway?" The angels wish we'd be more precise in our usage.

No doubt, as we move through Life's Elementary School Cafeteria Line, we would prefer to load our Tray of Experience with fish sticks and tater tots and ice cream sandwiches. Yet the Celestial Cafeteria Ladies, glowering at us from beneath their Divine Hair Nets, insist on giving us servings of lima beans and spinach and yes, sometimes even the frightening cauliflower. They say it is for our own good. And who are we to argue?

The Angels of
Humiliation

～～～～～～～～～～～～～～～～～～～～～～～～～

⌒

A great writer once said that if acclaim is the yeast in one's beer, humiliation is the pimento in one's olive. There is no way to have one without the other. Embrace humiliation! Go, dare, do, be! Reach, dream, run, smile! Flex, bake, tweeze, wink! The angels applaud from the sidelines.

⌒

～～～～～～～～～～～～～～～～～～～～～～～～～

The Angel on the F Train

My friends Clarabelle and Bob were typical young Brooklynites: they worked in Manhattan, boasted about their cheap rent, and collapsed in exhaustion at the end of each day's commute. But that was before an encounter with the Angels from Hell forever changed their attitudes about the train ride into the city.

It was a brisk fall morning, blue of sky and crisp of air. But both Clarabelle and Bob were blind to the celestial ribbons tied around their precious day. They woke up late, scalded their throats with coffee, and hurriedly, obliviously, dressed for the day ahead.

They rushed to the subway station and boarded

the crowded rush-hour F train. There were no seats, and both stood, grasping the silvery handrails over-head.

Suddenly, from the other end of the car came an impassioned cry: "Hey, lady!"

Heads turned toward the wizened old woman, who again called out, with some urgency: "Lady! Hey, lady!"

Clarabelle awoke from her stupor, feeling deep in her soul that somehow this message was meant for her. She turned, and the old woman's eyes bored into hers with a burning intensity. The old woman nodded.

"Yeah, you, lady! You got your ass hangin' out all over the subway!"

Startled, amazed, Clarabelle turned. Yes, the back of her skirt was tucked into its own waistband, and her posterior, clad only in semi-opaque tights with a substantial run in the left thigh, was exposed to the bleary-eyed gaze of the commuting throng.

Clarabelle yanked her skirt into position, then turned back to the woman. But she had disappeared!

Astounded, Clarabelle turned to Bob. He had

witnessed the event, and he was appalled. "I can't believe she just yelled that at you! In front of everybody!"

"Well, if you'd noticed it yourself and told me before we left the apartment, she wouldn't've *had* to yell at me."

"What, am I supposed to run a butt check on you every morning? Why didn't *you* notice? Didn't it seem a little drafty back there?"

Suddenly, staring at the glittery golden angel pinned to the rather formidable bosom (not Bob's) pressed in her face, Clarabelle experienced a moment of transcendent understanding. She realized that she had, in fact, just been visited by her Angels from Hell.

"I know I would've noticed if my skirt had been messed up all along. I mean, I'm not *that* much of a zombie in the morning. Or if I am, it's just because I have to come all the way in on that stupid train. No, it was my Angels from Hell. They tucked my skirt in, and then one of them took human form and yelled at me in the subway, just to show me, once and for all, what a jerk Bob is. I mean, it had been building up, but that was it. And $950 for a real one-bedroom with an eat-in kitchen is a great deal, but who needs it if you have to deal with a putz like Bob to get it?"

Cathy now has a tiny, insanely overpriced studio apartment of her own in Manhattan, and she can sleep an extra hour every morning. And she is happy. For this, she thanks her Angels from Hell.

"I feel so special. I mean, they went to all that trouble, just to send me a message. And I'll always be grateful."

Sometimes, the lessons we need to learn are like those mimes that seemed to be everywhere a few years ago—the ones who would follow us as we walked by, imitating us and making faces behind our backs and waving to passersby, all of whom could see what was going on and would start smirking and giggling while we just went on minding our own business, unaware of what everyone thought was so damn funny, anyway.

And sometimes not.

❋

No one can embarrass a cockroach.

❋

There is no humiliation in failing, coming up short, not measuring up, making that giant leap and falling flat on our faces. Humiliation exists only when other people are watching.

❋

Sometimes it may seem to us that our lives are simply a string of small humiliations interrupted occasionally by episodes of extreme mortification. And sometimes this is perfectly true.

The Salad Spinner of Humiliation exists to extract the gritty rinse-water of Hubris from the crunchy Romaine Lettuce of our Eternal Souls. And just who do you think is cranking the handle of that salad spinner?

"Tee-hee! Tee-hee-hee-hee! Tee-hee!" The angels are laughing—not *at* you, but *with* you.

The Angels Hit
the Beach

My dear friend Wynetta experienced a harrowing, yet heartwarming encounter with her Angels from Hell.

During her freshman year of college, Wynetta became involved with a fellow student named Smithers Mather Smythe IV. Known by his childhood nickname of Smidge, the young man was descended from a long line of blue-blooded Puritans, as one could readily guess from his diffident, self-effacing manner, his habit of blinking rapidly, and his pronounced lack of melanin.

Matters between Smidge and Wynetta progressed to the point that he thought it appropriate to extend an invitation to spend two weeks of the summer vacation at the family's vacation "cottage" on Nantucket ("Just an old pile, really; nothing fancy. And you know Dads and Mum and Corky think you're tops!").

Wynetta accepted with outward sangfroid and inward terror. Her own family traced its lineage back two generations to a trailer park in Bogalusa, Louisiana, and she found Dads, Mum, and Corky (Smidge's sister) about as comforting and cuddly as a trio of visitors from Planet Zorg. Smidge once had taken her to dinner at the family home, and Wynetta had been virtually paralyzed with anxiety and bewilderment. There was no Astroturf in sight. Alcoholic beverages were poured from decanters into glasses, rather than from aluminum cans into gullets. Dinner table conversation proceeded in a quiet and orderly fashion, with no sports arguments, no fighting over drumsticks, and absolutely no good-natured noogies, affectionate Dutch rubs, or loving fisticuffs.

During the first week of her visit to Nantucket, Wynetta crept about the family compound as if she were applying for the position of resident phantom. She barely spoke, flinching whenever she trod upon a squeaky floorboard and jumping outright whenever someone asked her to pass the salt, please. Even Nantucket's sugary sands and wavy waves brought Wynetta no joy. She simply lay in a deck chair, as relaxed as raw linguini, and wondered when she'd be asked to leave.

Perhaps it was the tension. Perhaps it was the diet of boiled items favored by the New England upper crust. Whatever the reason, Wynetta's digestive system declared a strike. Its glorious assortment of ducts and tubes and glands, so like a squishy and glistening modern dance company with really good choreography, simply shut down.

After seven days, Wynetta was in some distress. However, she was far too embarrassed to discuss her situation with any member of the family. She had the vague impression that the entire Smythe clan had made other arrangements in the bodily functions department—servants, consultants, perhaps a dispensation from God. She suffered in silence.

By the latter part of the weekend, Wynetta was desperate. She volunteered to drive into town for the Sunday paper, praying that once there, she'd find some potion to relieve her distress. From the shabby store shelves, a cobalt blue bottle beckoned. She purchased the *New York Times* and the bottle and shuffled back to the car. The directions on the bottle suggested a dose of two teaspoons, but Wynetta's Angels from Hell swung into action. They whispered persuasively in her ear, convincing her that if two teaspoons was good, four teaspoons was twice as good, eight was four times as good, and the entire bottle was best of all. Wynetta glugged away and tossed the empty bottle in the parking lot trash barrel. She drove back to the Smythe abode, feeling as if she'd just consumed a chalk smoothie, but confident of imminent relief.

After Sunday brunch, as planned, *la famille* Smythe *et* Wynetta piled into the station wagon for a visit to Bruce, the son of family friends. He and his longtime companion, Brice, had just finished renovating their cottage, and they were eager to show it off. A mile or two down the road, Wynetta felt the first intimations of an incipient intestinal inferno. By the time they'd arrived at their destination, the inferno was raging out of control.

On being introduced to Bruce and Brice, Wynetta's response was "Sonicetomeetyouwhere's the bathroom?" After a brief but eventful interlude, Wynetta rejoined the group for a tour of the house. She registered only random details of the home's transformation: antique paneling salvaged from a Vermont mapling shed, a collection of 1950s cocktail aprons transformed into café curtains, switchplates modeled on Toltec jaguar-god masks. She focused with great intensity on the three bathrooms, calculating and re-calculating with each step which facility was closest.

After Wynetta's eighth visit to the bathroom, everyone in the group—even her beloved Smidge— was looking at her with the slightly walleyed gaze of someone alarmed, puzzled, possibly even irritated by your behavior, but far too well-bred (or passive-aggressive) to say a word about it.

After a rather difficult night, Wynetta awoke exhausted and utterly renewed.

"It couldn't get any worse," she says. "What the hell." She taught everyone to play seven-card stud, and unabashedly won $13.78. She took over the kitchen and made gumbo for supper. She drank beer out of the bottle. She thoroughly enjoyed the remainder of her visit. And she's never allowed a sense of inferiority to interfere with her well-being again.

"The consequences are just too horrible," she says.

A human lifetime lasts but the span of a burp during Eternity's prix fixe dinner.

We all have awoken trembling from a nightmare in which we arrive at the office having somehow forgotten to get dressed, recognizing our nakedness only as we stand there next to coffee machine, displayed before our coworkers in all our flabby and fluorescent-lit glory. What can this universal dream of humiliation mean?

Simply this—it's never so bad that it can't get worse.

✳

"Peek-a-boo! We see you!" This is what the angels cry.

✳

Life is a party, and we must simply hope and trust and pray that it's not Lisette Gretzbach's Valentine's Day party—the one with the big, lacy, heart-shaped invitations she distributed before class, skipping about with her blonde ponytail bouncing merrily as she presented a fat shiny envelope to every single person in the room but you.

✳

"Fool" spelled backwards is "loof."

The Angels Cross the Big Pond

My lovely friend Mehitabel—who *is* remarkably attractive, especially for someone from England—shared this next story with me.

One Sunday afternoon, Mehitabel was piloting her laughably small English car back to London from a trip home to visit her parents. While passing through a thatchily twee and fiercely quaint village called Sloshing-on-Snit or Upper Toodle-Pip or Dinky Wad o' Lumpkin, she halted at the pedestrian crosswalk (or "zebra"). Two ladies of quality were proceeding grandly across the road, cleaving the soft country air with their beaklike noses and jutting bosoms, looking remarkably like two tweed-clad steamships sailing for a tea-shop port.

As the duo cleared Mehitabel's car hood (okay, "bonnet"), unforeseen disaster befell one of the women, demonstrating that the power of the Angels from Hell respects no national boundaries. In the twinkling of an eye, the worthy's capacious bloomers plummeted unceremoniously to the pavement, fluttering there like a smallish parachute emblazoned with teeny pink roses. The mortified matron froze in mid-stride.

Her companion, however, possessed the indominatible spirit that bore the Union Jack around the globe for so many years, at least until all that spotted dick and mushy peas and poor dental hygiene finally did its work and everyone had to go home and take advantage of their system of socialized medicine. As if chivvying a balky hunter over a jump, this Pearl of the Empire bellowed, "Step out of 'em, Ida! Step out of 'em, old girl!"

Ida rallied and stepped as bidden. Her companion, wielding a "brolly" with skill and élan, speared the bloomers and tossed them into her shopping bag. The two ships sailed on, no doubt headed home to bully their undersized husbands into writing apoplectically incoherent letters to the *Guardian* deploring the unmistakable postwar decline and current abominable state of the elastic in ladies' unmentionables.

Mehitabel was much impressed by this performance, and felt her pride in her countrymen renewed. "Dead brill!" she says. "Haven't had such a laugh in yonks! Wouldn't have thought the bags had it in 'em!"

Gravity is the personal assistant of humiliation.

So often, what we experience as humiliation is only the necessary twinge of a soul that is limbering up, preparing us for greater challenges, grander feats, unexpected changes of address.

※

We are such cowardly, craven, squishy souls, all a-tremble and a-quake at the notion that others might think badly of us, that we may embarrass ourselves in front of others. Yet we must remember that for "others," we ourselves are the "others," so in fact "we" and "others" are "one."

※

You can't hide under the covers forever.

※

Once again, we can rearrange the letters of the word "humiliation" for answers. Within it, we find "a lithium ion," which may suggest one treatment for extreme humiliation. And "Ma, hi, I oil nut," which presents a chirpy, humble and soul-tinglingly grand resolution to move forward and make the best of whatever menial and humiliating task the Divine Presence with the Cruel Sense of Humor sets for us.

The Angels of
Irritation

We have so many lessons to learn, and our teachers are everywhere. Even irritation is a teacher—the one you had in sixth grade who wore a leash on her glasses and applied lipstick all the way up to her nostrils and seemed obsessed with the "atomic bum" that flattened Hiroshima. Or so the angels say.

The Angels Teach a Dairy Valuable Lesson

While in college, my friend Ernie's brief tenure at a grocery store introduced him to the all-pervasive power of his Angels from Hell.

Ernie toiled as a stockboy—a position that suited him well, because it meant that he worked late at night, after the store was closed, when he and the other stockboys could blast Rush and King Crimson and Yes throughout the cavernous shrine to commerce while they slashed at cartons of cat food with macho vigor and engaged in fierce *mano a mano* bouts of air guitar.

But Ernie's merry world of late-night big-hair rock and filched Pop-Tarts came crashing down when the stock manager, the much-feared Mr.

Skaggs, assigned him to work in the much-loathed dairy section. It was dark back there, it was cold, and worst of all, the dairy restocking was done during the day. Not only would this require Ernie to be out of bed before four in the afternoon, but his first weekend on his new assignment threatened to interfere with a long-planned lake party, featuring weenie roasts and guitar sing-alongs and various wholesome hijinks.

Ernie was never one to search for the light peeping down through the dark and stormy clouds showering woe from above. He struggled against his fate with all the doomed valor of a teacup Yorkie approaching a romantically inclined St. Bernard. Ernie begged to trade shifts, but all his coworkers offered pathetically lame excuses such as, "I have to study," or "It's my girlfriend's birthday," or "My parents are in town." Mr. Skaggs himself was as unyielding as that foil thing that hermetically seals those cartons of orange juice with the little spigot on the side. He had only one response to Ernie's desperate pleas: "Quitcher bellyachin', son. You don't show up, you're fired."

Ernie did not want to lose his job, which financed necessities such as happy-hour pitchers, blank cassette tapes, and new six-packs of underpants that postponed the need to do laundry almost indefinitely. Supremely irritated, acknowledging defeat, he set four alarm clocks and resolved to appear in the dairy section promptly at the crack of noon that Saturday.

Once he arrived, the dairy section was far worse than Ernie's most lurid imaginings—a miasma of misery, an irrigation system of irritation. There was no place to play the tapes he'd brought. There were limited opportunities to wield the box-cutter. And his fellow workers were a dull, whey-faced bunch who didn't even laugh at his jokes about finally getting up close to Cream (Get it, cream, like, Cream?).

Again, Ernie tried to get out of his assignment. He coughed, he wheezed, he feigned appendicitis, he pleaded lactose intolerance. But Mr. Skaggs, a modern-day Simon Legree, ordered him to tote that quart, lift that tub! Consumed with curds of irritation, Ernie began to restock the cottage cheese display.

Irritation

From his vantage point, he could peer through the stacked dairy products and view the passing throngs of happy shoppers. An unsuspecting woman stopped before Ernie's domain. Possessed by infernal inspiration, Ernie grabbed a tub of cottage cheese (4% milkfat minimum). He thrust the mini-vat at her, wiggling it wildly and screeching in falsetto, "Buy *me!* Buy *me!* *I'm* the one! Take me *home!*"

The woman threatened a lawsuit, Ernie's fellow stockboys ratted him out, and Ernie was fired immediately. Now working as an investment banker, he looks back on this incident with fondness.

"That taught me to go with my gut," he says. "I should've just quit. Why [expletive deleted] around? Ba-da-bing, ba-da-boom—*done.* I learned something that day. Those angels, they're really on the ball."

※

No, life is not a bowl of cherries. Yet sometimes, if we search with diligence and perseverance and love in our heart, we find that life is indeed a bowl of nonfat cherry yogurt.

Angels from Hell

"Plinkplinkplinkplinkplinkplink*plinkplink plinkplinkplinkplink*plinkplinkplinkplinkplink plink*plink-plink-plink!*" The angels are playing "Chopsticks." Can you hear them?

Think of the last time you took in a huge fluffy breath of air and experienced the sensation that you've inhaled something—a fragment of fairy dust, or the rainbow-tinted residue of a wish, or a bit of pigeon fluff— something that your body, in its wisdom and its foolishness, refused to take on board. You sneezed and hacked and snorted fruitlessly for what seemed like an eternity, until finally you tried to ignore whatever it was and resume your normal life . . . only to be seized by another sneezing fit.

That's irritation.

❋

We cannot scratch an itch we cannot reach.

❋

Oh, what are we to do when the Prankster Above decides that we would benefit from an endless and irritating series of Metaphysical Knock-Knock Jokes?

72

What indeed?

The Angels Attend a Double Feature

As a perky young pixie, my dear friend Tallulah frequented a movie theater that specialized in double features of what were called (in that less exquisitively sensitive era) blaxploitation films. On this particular night, Tallulah had savored the neo-post-colonial epic *Shaft in Africa* and was eagerly awaiting *Black Mama, White Mama*, with its overtones of Manichean neo-expressionism.

In the interim, two young women seated in front of Tallulah began a highly animated discussion, conducted at a pitch and volume sufficient to penetrate lead walls. The maidens compared notes on the remarkable physical attractiveness of a gentleman named Rayvon. They ranked their respective encounters with his superior (even Olympic caliber) athletic and acrobatic prowess. They described his astonishing physical endowments in both linear and volumetric terms. Much as they esteemed Rayvon, they loathed his significant other, Seychelle, and gleefully cataloged her social ineptitude, her fashion errors, and her lapses in personal hygiene.

At first, Tallulah and all within earshot were titillated. But quickly (as is so often its wily way!) titillation turned to boredom, and then to irritation. Within minutes, Tallulah feared that her ears would begin to bleed if she were forced to listen to any more.

Suddenly, from the back of the theater, came a ringing voice: "You are gettin' on my last black nerve! Why don't you just shut your mouth, niche*?"

The entire theater fell silent.

After a long moment, one of the maidens said, loudly, "I know no one's gonna call me 'niche' to my face."

*The actual word used was slightly different, although quite similar. Since this is intended as a family publication offering spiritual guidance and sustenance suitable for all ages, however, you'll just have to use your imagination.

All eyes swiveled in their sockets to observe the response. A woman rose from the back row and took her stance in the aisle. Stout in frame and spirit, one sensed that she had seen much and tolerated little. Gazing upon the woman, Tallulah felt a chill, a tingle, a *frisson*. Her rational mind said, "Your foot's fallen asleep." But her fluttery soul cried, "It's an Angel—an Angel from Hell!"

The Angel glared fiercely and planted her right fist at her hip. Girding herself with her steely, sturdy aura, she marched forward in majestic cadence, heedless of the squashed Milk-Duds, flattened jujubes, and splayed popcorn kernels in her path.

And in dreadful, chilling, hypnotic rhythm with her march, she intoned, "Niche . . . [stomp] . . . Niche . . . [stomp] . . . Niche." Inexorably, the Angel advanced toward her prey—and as she advanced, throughout the theater, fearful heads sank below seat level, teeny hairs bristled along spines, male generative organs retracted within body cavities. And all the while: "Niche . . . [stomp] . . . Niche . . . [stomp] . . . Niche."

Irritation

As the tension reached a chaotic crescendo—as the chilling chant reached its perilous peak, as the venomous virago reached for her prey's gleaming jhericurls—the theater went dark. The projector warbled to life, and soon the preview of coming attractions (*The Thing With Two Heads*, featuring sensitive and highly nuanced performances by Ray Milland and Rosie Grier in the title role) filled the screen. Disaster was averted.

Tallulah has never forgotten the lesson she learned that day. "Every time I catch myself entertaining a captive audience with details of my private life, I remember that Angel from Hell, and that look on her face. And I just shut right up."

❈

Sssshhhh! Not so loud! The angels were out late, and they're a bit hung over and cranky.

❈

There is much we can learn in the course of a long car trip with an esteemed relative who derives great pleasure from the small things in life—such as reading aloud all the signs along the road and following each recitation with a guttural exhalation of surprise. Listen to the litany of joy and wonder: "'Kwik-Dry.' Heh. . . . 'East Main Street.' Heh. . . . 'No Right Turn.' Heh. . . . 'Max. Load 2000 Lbs.' Heh. . . . 'IH-10 West.' Heh. . . ." And what we learn from this is that next time we must purchase plane tickets well in advance.

Irritation is the soul's eczema.

Many, many, many, many years ago, penitents wrapped themselves in sad and unflattering garments woven of itchy and unwashed hair gathered from our mammal friends. They offered up the resulting unbearable irritation to The Great Otherness Above.

Today, we can accomplish the same thing by listening to talk radio.

How are we to react when we pour a Cup of Spiritual Coffee and add the Milk of Emotion, only to discover that the Milk of Emotion is curdled and floats in repugnant little clumps in our now-ruined Cup of Spiritual Coffee? Hard to say, but one thing is certain—we must not let our disappointment and irritation spur us into resorting to the Non-Dairy Creamer of Bland Pop-Culture Response.

The Angels Decide Turnabout Is Fair Play

Many years ago, I became acquainted with the members of a modern-day salon of sorts: a group of young and impecunious sculptors, painters, performance artists, substance abusers, and other unemployables. The merry band took over a cavernous warehouse in the industrial section of a large Gulf Coast city. Working in the true spirit of artistic camaraderie, they bickered incessantly, drank themselves insensible, and (despite their feckless efforts) eventually managed to convert the echoing raw space into a self-indulgent young artiste's Valhalla—grotty studios, highly unsanitary living spaces, and an art gallery and performance space fully outfitted with sophomoric pretension and bohemian snobbery.

Of all the colorful and unstable personalities who inhabited the warehouse, Heathcliff was by far the most remarkable. Though born and raised in Pillbug, Oklahoma, Heathcliff spoke in an impeccable tennis-whites-and-tee-off lockjaw, delivered in fluting, quavering tones that occasionally sailed above the range of human hearing. (Imagine Thurston Howell crossed with Truman Capote, inhaling helium.) Heathcliff drank wine coolers by the gallon, sipping from a brass plant hanger suspended from his neck in the manner of a sommelier's cup. Heathcliff provoked fistfights with the neurotic, cuticle-gnawing girls who lurked about the warehouse, persisting in this habit even after being thrashed rather severely more than once. Heathcliff fancied himself the resident critic for all performances that took place at the warehouse; just before the close of the first act of an experimental light-opera version of *No Exit,* he took the stage and urinated on the front row of spectators, which observers agreed was an extreme case of blaming the victim. In short, Heathcliff was an intensely irritating creature. Five minutes in Heathcliff's company awakened in the most pacific soul an urge to clonk him in the head with a brick.

In the wee-est hours of one morning, the rail spur behind the warehouse became the scene of a minor mishap—and Heathcliff's comeuppance at the hands of his Angels from Hell. On that night, the latches on several boxcars containing petrochemical something-or-other gave way, spilling heaps of waxy white pellets to the ground. Heathcliff was still awake (or at least ambulatory) when this occurred. Drawn by the clamor, he wandered out to observe the action.

A special unit of the fire department had been dispatched for the task of cleaning up, and the men were earnestly shoveling the detritus into bins. At first, Heathcliff sought to encourage their labors by singing "Old Man River." That entertainment palled quickly, however, as the men did nothing but glare and mutter.

Then Heathcliff squinched his eyes shut, thrust his hands forward, and stomped toward the crew in the manner of Boris Karloff, warbling in his distinctive voice, "I've beeeeeeen in a chemicallllll spiiiiiill! Aaaaagh! I've been bliiiiiiinded! I've beeeeen in a chemicalllll spiiiiiiiill!"

The response from the fire department was not as gratifying as he'd hoped. Profanities figured prominently, and one railroad spike was hurled in his direction, but there was no full-scale riot. Heathcliff retreated to the warehouse—routed, but not defeated.

He soon reappeared, his face glowing ghostly white, fizzing with eerie foam. Again, he began his haunting cry: "I've beeeeeeeeen in a chemicalllllll spiiiiiiill! Aaaaaaaooooooohhhh!!!!"

The firefighters gaped at him, appalled and aghast. Had this crazy sumbitch somehow managed to injure himself? Would they be held liable? While they were pondering the possibilities, Heathcliff's cries suddenly sharpened. He began clawing at his cheeks, wailing ever more loudly. He had smeared his face with toothpaste to simulate an encounter with noxious chemicals, and now something in the formulation—the fluoride, the saccharine, or perhaps the minty-fresh flavor—was irritating his sensitive skin.

Heathcliff's piteous cries awakened his fellow artisans, all of whom were delighted to discover his plight. While Heathcliff writhed under the garden hose behind the warehouse, his *compadres,* laughing uproariously at his agonies, brought a few beers out to the cleanup crew. The laborers and the layabouts shared many a chuckle—a delightful and unlikely fellowship brought about by Heathcliff's own Angels from Hell.

Irritation is like an emery board—it works both ways.

What are we to learn from that niggling, nagging sensation—a feeling that in the Great Garment of Life, there is hidden some remnant

of the Psychic Price Tag, or an especially scratchy Supreme Garment-Maker's Label, or even a stray Straight Pin from the Seamstress of Us All? What, indeed?

Only this—that sometimes, the Divine Nail Scissors can be put to another (perhaps higher) use.

So many, many times, life is like a faucet that works perfectly well for a long, long time. So well and so long, in fact, that we don't even think about its beauty and complexity and melancholy necessaryness until that faucet begins to drip, drip, drip . . . refusing to cease no matter how hard we twist the knob thing, just drip, drip, drip . . . all night long while we lie in bed with a pillow over our head.

Before we bid farewell to our friend Irritation, let us once again consult the oracle contained in the inscrutable word itself. And lo, we find two sparkling fireworks expressing the springy indomitability of the human spirit: "Ain't I it, Orr?" and "Tart I, in Rio."

The Angels of
Boredom

~~~~~~

ᏹ

There is a stillness at the center of Being, a stillness that unenlightened souls call "boredom," "tedium," "ennui," or "watching the paint dry." The enlightened know that this quiet pond is where the algae grow thickest, greenest, bubbliest. The angels know this, too.

ᏹ

~~~~~~

The Angels Solve
for X

An ex-boyfriend once told me about a particularly
memorable algebra lesson taught by his Angels from
Hell.

Like many of us, Basil struggled mightily to ap-
prehend the symmetry and beauty of higher mathe-
matics, to no avail. Throughout tenth grade, algebra
remained inelegant gibberish, a mishmash of letters
and tiny numbers—a box of Alpha-Bits gone utterly,
tragically mad.

The teacher, Mr. Nesbit, offered little inspiration, though he tried his best. He was a game, if chin-
less, fellow, with an unfortunate habit of snaking one
hand up the opposite shirt sleeve to scratch vigor-
ously at his armpit while exhorting the class to "solve

Boredom

for *X!*" The class took place during fifth period, when the soporific effect of the Frito pies and sloppy joes was at its zenith. Day after day, Algebra I was a Philip Glass-ian symphony of chalk squeaking, Mr. Nesbit scritching, and dozing heads thunking against laminated desktops.

As far as Basil was concerned, the only bright spot in the class was the fact that he'd been assigned a seat next to Mona Fink—or "Moana," as Basil secretly thought of her. She was blindingly beautiful and wildly popular, and of course Basil had no delusions that she'd ever deign to notice a lowly weasel such as himself. Between catnaps, he was happy simply to bask in the aura of her incandescent beauty.

Imagine, then, Basil's surprise when Moana actually *smiled* at him! It happened during one especially dull lesson when, for his own amusement, Basil drew a perhaps unkind caricature of Mr. Nesbit emitting puffy clouds of algebraic equations from his hindparts. Basil heard a silvery giggle, and looked up to see Moana smiling at him. Emboldened, he drew more and more outlandish pictures, much to the delight of his *amour.*

"That was when the Angels from Hell took over," Basil says. He felt inspired to further entertain Moana with the only props he had at hand: a half-eaten bag of peanut M&Ms. He selected the largest candy—a green one, as it happened—and inserted it into his right nostril, thus displaying (he hoped) an alluring, madcap *joie de vivre*.

Moana giggled blondely, and Basil—flushed with twinkly success—tried to remove the crunchy confection. But, alas, it refused to budge. His increasingly frantic snorting and huffing served only to lodge the swinish sweet more firmly, and his explosive thrashings awakened the rest of the class and arrested Mr. Nesbit in mid-scritch. All eyes were upon Basil as the snide snack at last relinquished its place, melting into a chocolately rivulet that cascaded from his nostril, along his upper lip, and down his chin. The peanut, stripped of its sugary shroud, plopped onto Basil's desk with a soft yet resonant *plink!*

"Moana never looked at me again," Basil recalls. "Plus, I got a D in algebra. And for a long time, I thought this was just another one of those things that you spend a lot of time talking about in therapy later on. But then, when I'd been in college two or three years, and I was getting a lot of pressure to pick a major, for some reason I just thought about that algebra class. And it was like I heard a voice: 'Stick to drawing, moron!' And that was it."

Basil is now a poor but happy painter, with a loving (if slightly exasperated) girlfriend who has a real job. And he's certain he owes it all to his Angels from Hell.

"Sweets for the sweet"—or so the saying goes. There's another saying: "Candy's dandy, but liquor's quicker." Hmmmm.

Nothing under the dreamy blue upside-down popcorn bowl of Heaven is as blissful as sneaking a quick nap in a really boring meeting. Except, possibly, watching someone else snooze peacefully and begin to drool on his tie.

Why does boredom make our eyelids so heavy? Ha! We may as well ask why does the grass grow, why is the sky blue, why does the bird fly, why does the dog shed so damn much all year round, why is there never anything good on TV, and why is the checking account balance always less than it ought to be? Ha!

Sometimes, all we need is a nap.

Those clever, saucy angels! Within the very word "boredom," they offer antidotes to spongy tepid tedium: not only "bed moo" but also "Rob, do me." Oh, the vampy wisdom of the angels—it brings tears of gratitude to the happy eye.

The Angels Pursue Higher Learning

A dear girlfriend related this angel story to me.

Gelsomina had only one ambition in life: to become a professor of English. She longed to inculcate in eager young scholars the fervent love of the riches of literature—the transgressive fervor of "The Charge of the Light Brigade," the searing passion of *Adam Bede,* the scathing post-structural critique of Eurocentric values inherent in "One Fish, Two Fish." Plus, she thought it would be really cool to have all that time off.

In her first year of graduate school, Gelsomina was granted an assistantship, which meant that she would at last realize her dream of teaching. Conditions for her first foray into the classroom were admittedly less than ideal; she was assigned to teach freshman composition, and her class met at eight in the morning on Monday, Wednesday, and Friday. But Gelsomina was undaunted.

She worked feverishly, developing hip and relevant lessons from articles in *Details* magazine; preparing an incisive and witty analysis of the poetic structure of "Smells Like Teen Spirit"; purchasing important and forthright platform shoes. She drew on all media for her lesson plans: the written text, the spoken word, the music video, the sock puppet.

All to no avail.

By the end of her first week of teaching, she had evoked exactly two questions from her class: "Is this on the mid-term?" and "How late can we drop?" Day after day, Gelsomina faced an array of faces as blank as English muffins, all lavishly buttered with boredom.

Finally, a month into the semester, something clicked. Gelsomina walked into the classroom, faced the panoply of Pantera and Bart Simpson T-shirts, and began her lesson. And the class paid attention! The snoozing louts of Monday were tranformed into the rapt scholars of Wednesday. Amazed, delighted,

Gelsomina grew more animated and more effusive, gesticulating with the verve and élan of a latter-day Martha Graham. And the class followed her every move.

All aglow with pedagogical triumph, Gelsomina bid her students adieu until Friday. She had underestimated them. What perception! What focus! What dedication! She pondered their many fine qualities as she made her way to the graduate student lounge and the ladies' restroom therein. She caught sight of herself in the mirror, and could not help but notice that the third button on her '70s-retro blouse had popped open, displaying her not-quite-white brassiere with its broken front clasp and the large safety pin she used in place of said clasp.

Gelsomina did show up for class on Friday, but it was a new Gelsomina. She assigned homework. She made them read from the textbook. She used overheads.

And today Gelsomina has nothing to do with teaching. "Do I look like an idiot?" she says. "That little incident opened my eyes but good. Those kids were bored out of their tiny little minds, and, quite frankly, I was, too—I'm just not cut out for school." She's now a scuba-diving arc welder on offshore oil rigs, and she's happy.

All thanks to her Angels from Hell.

Often, when our alarm clock goes off, we want only to ask, "Why?"

Each minute we stay awake in the face of crushing boredom earns us an unlimited credit at the Great Bergdorfs Above, or perpetual center-court seats in the Stadium On High—our choice.

That's what we can tell ourselves, anyway.

One could say, "Let sleeping dogs lie." Or, "Let lying dogs sleep." Or, "Set leaping logs die." Or, "Debt bleeping frogs sigh."

＊

What we, in our gibbering earthly foolishness, call "boredom" is actually the angels' offering of rest and respite and relaxation, a brief visit to a spa without the smudge sticks or the paper panties or the horrifying bill afterward. Oh, the softly sparkling generosity of those angels!

The Angels Grant a Wish

This is a precious and well-loved tale, told and re-told in the family of my friend Clarence.

When Clarence's Uncle Dink was a mere stripling, large of Adam's apple and scrawny of chest, a distant relation found a summer job for him with the Southern Pacific Railroad. In those long-ago days, the railroad had the same glamour, the same cachet, the same whiff of cutting-edgeness that we now associate with the Internet and Andrew Lloyd Webber musicals. In the days before Uncle Dink reported for work, he dreamed of faraway places, swashbuckling adventures, beautiful women weeping brokenheartedly and begging him for help, fast women smoking cigarettes and begging him for other things.

As so often happens in this imperfect world, however, reality did not measure up to Dink's dreams. He was assigned to the railyard, re-tarring boxcar roofs. The disadvantages of the job were many. The task offered woefully limited opportunities for travel and adventure. There were no women—beautiful, fast, or otherwise—in sight. The southern sun sizzled down, searing and singeing the skin of his shoulders and scalp. The tar fumes stung his eyes. But worst of all was the boredom.

Each evening, Dink returned home and complained to his mother about the vast expanses of sticky, black nothing that filled his day. Splotch, swab, splotch, swab—this was the only action in sight. Each evening, he would wail, "I just wish somethin' would happen!" And each evening, his mother would warn, "You watch what you wish for, Dink. You just might get it."

Dink became more and more demoralized, dozing later and later in bed, dawdling later and later over breakfast. Finally, one blistering August morning, Dink managed to sleep through breakfast altogether. When he awoke at last, Dink dressed in a frenzied panic and (with his mother practically heaving him through the screen door) raced to the railyard.

Atop the boxcar, the adrenaline rush of the morning drained away and Dink nearly dozed as he squatted at his tar bucket: splotch, swab, splotch, swab. Insects hummed and buzzed. Heat waves shivered and shimmered. And then, just as Dink had wished, something happened—the back seam of his trousers split. In his morning frenzy, Dink had neglected to don underpants, and his goolies (as our British cousins would say), his *huevos* (as they're known South of the Border), his orbs of joy (as a charming Eastern European idiom has it) dropped onto the tar roof of the boxcar, that sticky black surface all a-sizzle in the summer sun.

The story has entered family lore, along with Uncle Dink's mother's wise admonition, "You watch what you wish for. You just might get it." An unforgettable lesson taught by the Angels from Hell.

If you can't stand the heat, turn on the air-conditioning.

104

When our lives are filled with drumming tedium, like a Wurlitzer with its rhythm setting stuck on mambo; when we feel ourselves trudging across a trackless plain of dullness, like an ant traversing a pie pan; when there is nothing to break the yawning expanse of meaningless work, joyless relationships, and unendurable ennui—it is then that we must count our blessings and tell ourselves things could be worse.

We *could* be dung beetles.

Don't think of it as boredom. Think of it as a very low-tech form of meditation.

Occasionally (most often during after-lunch seminars in stuffy, overheated rooms) our boredom reaches a state of tedious transcendence, and our consciousness unfetters itself from our lumpen and loaflike selves. In our reveries, our sprightly spirits frolic on tropical isles, romp through the size-2 racks and find the frocks too large, and deliver a withering and spine-crushing harangue that leaves our moronic reptile of a boss writhing on the cheap office carpeting like a salt-sprinkled slug. And always, our Angels from Hell are with us. We know this because our return ticket from the fantasy land of Über-Boredom invariably is a booming voice that says, "And what do *you* think about that, [insert your name here]?"

A watched clock never moves.

The Angels of Frustration

Nothing is more frustrating than frustration. Indeed, the word "frustration" is itself frustrating. Just look at it—all crumpled and squinched-looking and just too long and frustrating. Yet it must hold secrets for us to discover. What can they be? The angels are passing us notes.

My Very Own Angel Story

When I was a mere sprig on the Tree of Life, a tender girlish bundle of blushes and giggles and inexplicable weeping fits, I had a most memorable encounter with my Angels from Hell.

In those long-ago days of women's liberation and *Charlie's Angels*, schoolgirls spent hours and hours and hours together in loving sisterhood, tenderly brushing out each others' hair until each head was a shining sheet of gleamingness. Sadly, I was excluded from this demi-chthonic ritual. I possess hair of such profusion of thickness and vibrancy of texture that my fellow sixth-graders dubbed me "Rat's Nest" in its honor. No brush can conquer it; combs quiver at its approach.

My hair, quite frankly, ruined my life. I spent hour upon frustrating hour trying to spin my frowsy brunette straw into silky blonde gold. I purchased all the magazines catering to persons just entering the full flower of womanhood; at that time, all advocated a "natural" approach, which involved filching items from the kitchen and adapting them to cosmetic purposes—cucumber eye soothers, oatmeal facial masques, and the like. I focused on the problem-hair suggestions, especially those in the "dry, frizzy" category. These adages advocated slathering one's locks with mayonnaise, eggs, olive oil, and other greasy substances.

I tried all these potions faithfully, but my hair remained frustratingly brown and wiry. I wept, I slammed doors, I sulked, I drummed my heels on the floor, I threatened suicide. And at last, my Angels from Hell answered—"Your hair is extraordinarily bad; therefore, it requires extraordinary measures. If olive oil is good, then Crisco is better."

Yes, I concocted a hot-shortening treatment. After a lengthy shower, I smeared my hair with hydrogenated vegetable oil, wrapped my head in polyethylene film, and topped the entire structure with a hot towel for a half-hour deep conditioning session. As I was rinsing off, I noted that my hair felt, well, *weird*. Not knowing how "real" hair felt, however, I assumed that this deep-fat-fried feeling was absolutely normal. I wrapped my hair in the requisite orange-juice-can rollers and clanked off to bed.

The next morning dawned with the birds all a-twitter, the oatmeal all a-burble, and my mother all a-screech, yelling at my brother to get out of bed and turn off that damn clock-radio already, does he want us all to go deaf listening to that G.D. noise.* I leapt up, eager to view my newfound follicular fabulosity.

When I unleashed my hair from the rollers, each curl clung fiercely to its cylindrical shape. Yes, I could get a comb through it, but the result was a strangely lumpy spectacle, as if many tiny mammals had smeared themselves with sunblock and crowded onto my head to bask. Horrified, I tried to coax my

*In the interests of familial harmony, I should point out that this depiction is grossly exaggerated for comic effect. My mother actually is a very sweet, well-mannered woman who would never engage in such behavior. I mean it. Really, she's not anything like this at all. My *father*, on the other hand . . .

hair into some semblance of its normal, shrublike form, but to no avail. The Crisco had lent it a resilience that rendered it unresponsive to water, to mousse, to setting gel, to pretty much anything short of an oxyacetylene torch. I was forced to go to school looking like the love child of James Brown and Little Orphan Annie.

I wish I could say that the resulting horrors—the averted eyes, the uproarious laughter, the swarming insects—taught me to appreciate my hair as the God(dess) of Nature created it. But no. I went through several more years of uneasy giant-roller dreams followed by early-morning struggles with blow dryers, curling irons, hot rollers, and styling mousse before I fully assimilated the lesson my Angels were trying to teach me: If it cuts into your sleep, it's not worth it.

※

Frustration is to joy as sandpaper is to finishing rinse.

"Pfzzt! Sszztzzzt! Ssszzzzzzzz! Pfzzt! Pfzzt! Sszztzzzt!" The angels are fryin' up a mess of bacon. Can you smell it? No? Well, you could stand to lose a few pounds, anyway. And, besides, didn't you see *Babe*?

To see your angels, you have only to look up. Higher. A little to the left. No, not that far. Okay, now squint. More. *More*. Can't you see them yet? Well, try again. No, not *that* way. Oh, forget it.

Sometimes, as we traverse the Eternal Freeway, we find ourselves stuck between exits, in bumper-to-bumper Psychic Traffic.

When we curse and punch the Emotional Dash-
board, does the traffic flow faster? The Angels
think not.

꙳

When we unfold the lessons concealed in
the origami-ness of "frustration," what do we
find? A blessed gurgling fountain of a gift, in
the form of two forthright advisories from our
Angels from Hell: "Faint or rust," and "Fart ni-
trous." Ah, the divine and winking wiliness of
those angels!

The Angels Have a Dog-Gone Good Time

My dear friend Eugenie once fell madly in love with a strapping young man named, aptly enough, Claude. The Great Blackjack Dealer in the Sky had tossed some good cards Claude's way—as S/He does with us all, if we have but the wit to recognize when to hold and when to say "Hit me." Claude undoubtedly was decorative; he'd spruce up a sofa as well as any ten kilim pillows. He had a true talent for sopping up malt-based alcoholic beverages. He was also quite gifted in the sheer-bulk department; if you needed a jar opened or a piano moved or a safe dropped on someone's head, Claude was your man.

Claude's Blackjack Hand in Life, however, did not quite add up to twenty-one. It's doubtful that

Claude himself could add up to twenty-one. Claude was a simple soul, content with simple pleasures: cold beer, a warm television tuned to ESPN, and the company of his faithful dog, Spaz.

It was a match doomed from the start (Claude and Eugenie, not Claude and Spaz). Eugenie, while possessed of a quirky charm all her own, could never be described as the athletic type. She develops a rash when overheated. She tends to trip while walking on flat surfaces. She throws not merely like a girl, but like a girl squid. The life of the mind is the life for her, unless there's a good sale on at Macy's.

Nevertheless, Eugenie was determined to win Claude's heart. She attended his softball games, drank at his sports bars, screamed herself hoarse for his teams—basketball, football, and hockey. She spent countless hours at the driving range; at the batting cage; at the ballpark, the stadium, the arena; in the park watching Spaz chase tennis balls. (She wasn't allowed to throw the ball herself, because Spaz became confused and upset when he went long and the ball landed four feet in front of Eugenie's toes.)

Eugenie also sought to introduce Claude to the finer things in life, to lure him into her realm. At the time, she was going through a period of intense and rather annoying identification with Martha Stewart. She was forever bustling about tinting curtains with old coffee, or fashioning clever home accessories from duct tape, or stenciling seasonal designs on baseboards. Because Claude's taste in interior decorating ran mainly to cinder blocks and pizza boxes, Eugenie wisely limited her Martha-esque endeavors, Claude-wise, to the culinary sphere.

And so she broiled and braised, steamed and shirred, frappéd and fricasseed. She made tray after tray of individual meat loaves, each in the form of a regulation-size hockey puck. She baked six dozen Cornish pasties, shaping each one into a tiny football, complete with juliénned-potato laces. She created a Sacher-torte scale model of Madison Square Garden, complete with a maple-frosting court, tiny marzipan players, and teensy nets crocheted from licorice whips.

All of this effort added up to endless frustration. Claude (and Spaz) always partook heartily of these elaborate dishes, usually while watching the sporting event of the moment on Claude's big-screen TV. Claude always tossed her a "Thanks, doll" during a commercial break, and occasionally Spaz favored her with a gassy belch. That was it. She may as well have served beenie-weenies, or tuna casserole, or fluorescent-orange macaroni and cheese from a box.

A frustrated and despairing Eugenie resolved to outdo herself for Claude's Super Bowl party. It was an extra-special event that year, because the big game coincided with Spaz's birthday. Eugenie vetoed Claude's plan to head out to the Consume-A-Rama Wholesale Club for fifty pounds of chips, a drum of bean dip, and a bag of rawhide bones; instead, she volunteered to cater the gala. On Super Bowl eve, as Claude snoozed, Eugenie slaved away. All through the night and into the morning, she worked, creating a sumptuous array of fabulous dishes: venison and azuki bean chili, Calvados-glazed Cornish game hens, yellow-finn potatoes au gratin, eggs (from free-range and well-adjusted hens), *beurre noir*, various animal parts *en croute*.

The centerpiece was a birthday pâté Eugenie

created for Spaz. She had intended to roast a beef
haunch, grind the meat fine, season it with brewer's
yeast, bee pollen, and Vitamin E, and layer it with as-
pic infused with Bud Lite (Spaz's tipple of choice).
However, time ran short. At a certain point, a bleary-
eyed Eugenie found herself saying, "Screw it." She
drove to the nearest Stop-N-Rob, purchased six cans
of generic dog food, mixed in a few Livasnaps,
dumped it all on a platter, shaped it into a heart, and
called it a night.

The aforementioned feast dazzled even Claude.
When Eugenie arose, he greeted her with a heartfelt,
"Wow, cool chow. Huh. I'm a poet and din't even
know it."

Eugenie watched him fondly, wondering which
of the delicacies he would sample first. He strolled
back and forth, pondering his choices, until at last he
picked up a knife, selected a slice of organic
sprouted-rye bread, and slathered it with a generous
helping of Spaz's paté. Before Eugenie could say a
word, he'd scarfed down that morsel and was reach-
ing for another.

"That was it," Eugenie says. "It was like the Angels from Hell were trying to get my attention before, but then they just gave up and whanged me with a skillet. I mean, was I nuts, or what? Claude's a sweetie, but c'mon—I have about as much in common with him as with your average doorknob. Less, maybe."

Eugenie dressed, kissed Claude on the cheek (warily avoiding his pâté-smeared lips), said "You have a good time, honey," and fled to her apartment.

She has no regrets.

122

One man's meat is another man's *poisson*.

Sometimes the moment when we fight the hardest is the moment when we realize we are the strongest, if we pick sufficiently puny opponents.

If one finds oneself continually banging one's figurative head against one's metaphysical walls, then one should ask oneself what it is that oneself would like to accomplish, where oneself would like to be, whether oneself is being true and faithful to oneself, and what the hell oneself thinks one is doing, anyway.

An Angelic
Stage Show

In his younger days, my friend Lancelot worked as a bartender at a club known throughout the city for its drag shows. One evening, the stage was graced by one of the city's foremost drag queens, a formidable and flamboyant presence whom we'll call Lady Miss Lycra.

This downtown diva did not disappoint. She had all the stage presence that eight-inch platforms and 48-DDD falsies could provide, plus a set of pipes that could hail ships at sea. Rather than relying upon the more traditional lip-synching, Lady Miss Lycra sang every syllable herself, to great effect. As she belted out "Somewhere Over the Rainbow," there was scarcely a dry eye in the house.

Graciously, Lady Miss Lycra acceded to the

unanimous and uproarious calls for an encore. And that was when the Angels from Hell intervened.

Among the usual audience of multiply pierced and over-accessorized regulars, there sat a trio of tourists—corn-fed, apple-cheeked Midwestern girls. At first, they placidly enjoyed their walk (or seat) on the wild side. But just after Lady Miss Lycra returned to the stage, the smallest of the girls (still a sturdy specimen) exceeded her metabolic maximum of Long Island iced teas. Apparently under the delusion that she was in attendance at a choreographed karaoke event, she clambered up on stage and attempted to sing along with the star.

Our besieged heroine was, in almost every sense of the term, a true lady. She first tried to unobtrusively remove the intruder by bumping her repeatedly with her ample hip. The interloper staggered, but kept her feet. The miscreant's friends raced up and clutched at her ankles, to no avail. The toasted trollop tromped about the stage, wailing what seemed to be "Born in the U.S.A." transposed into some unknown key, utterly obliterating the diva's sensitive rendition of "A Tisket, A Tasket."

At last, Lady Miss Lycra lost her patience. Frustrated and fuming, she ended her number with a grand Al Jolson-esque flourish—backhanding the Swiss Miss right in the choppers.

Substantial as she was, the girl went flying. After all, Lady Miss Lyrca had not only sung with the Whiffenpoofs, she also had started on Yale's offensive line. The Blonde Bomber sailed over several chairs, skidded across a table, and landed atop a young fan's Josie and the Pussycats lunchbox/handbag, squashing it flat. (Ever one for the magnanimous gesture, Lady Miss Lycra later invited the tearful admirer to her home to select one of her very own bags as compensation.)

Dear Lancelot has summed up the lesson of this incident with beautiful clarity and poetry: "Never, ever try to upstage a drag queen."

※

Nothing is more frustrating than trying to squeeze a size-12 body into a size-6 dress—especially when the dress used to fit.

When the key breaks off in the lock; when we madly try to jam a left-hand foot into a right-hand shoe; when we spend an entire day in a sequence of lines at a government office, only to reach the head of the very last line and discover that we lack one vital (and heretofore unmentioned) document; when our eternal soul screams silently in scathing frustration— that is the moment to remember the glories of boredom.

Who are these mysterious beings who shower us with the magnificent gifts of frustration, loss, irritation, boredom, and humiliation? Why do they love us so dearly and persistently, like a swarm of otherworldly hornets? When can we expect them to go away? These questions are all part of the eternal mysteries of life.

Frustration

As we reel helplessly from one blighted day to the next, beseiged by the infernally ingenious Angels from Hell—buzz-bombed by gnat-like Irritation; choking in ether-ish clouds of Boredom; whipped into hypertensive fury by Frustration; staring blankly in the flummoxy wake of Loss; floundering in the queasy depths of Humiliation—it may occur to us to wonder what it all means, what our higher purpose may be, how we can make sense of the bewildering chaos that surrounds us. As we cogitate upon these conundrums, we may be assured of this— the answers we seek surely won't be found in a cheap paperback full of dim-witted platitudes and fatuous anecdotes

And if they are, we're in bigger trouble than we thought.